HOW TO BUILD A
HUG

Temple Grandin and Her Amazing Squeeze Machine

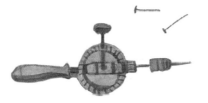

by Amy Guglielmo and Jacqueline Tourville

illustrated by Giselle Potter

Atheneum Books for Young Readers
New York London Toronto Sydney New Delhi

Temple loved folding paper kites,
making obstacle courses for her dog,
and building lean-tos with real hinged doors.

Temple did not like scratchy socks,
whistling teakettles, bright lights,
or smelly perfumes.

And Temple really didn't like hugs.

When other kids looked sad, lonely, or scared,
Temple could see that hugs cheered them up.
If people were grateful or really happy, they passed out hugs like cookies.
And holding your arms out wide usually meant you wanted a great big hug.

Temple wanted to be held, too.
But to her, hugs felt like being stuffed inside the scratchiest sock
in the world. If anyone tried to give her a hug, she kicked
and screamed and pulled away.

At school,
Temple wasn't like the other kids.

No one understood that when
the classroom fan WHIRRED,
Temple imagined a dentist's drill.

That to her, the voices in the loud,
stinky cafeteria ROARED
like a jet engine,

and the school bell CLANGED
like a woodpecker
knocking on her head.

To escape the noisy images,
Temple fled to the playground swings,

where she spun
and hummed
until the sounds vanished
in the breeze.

The wound-up
swing felt snug
and secure.
*Is this
what hugs
are supposed
to feel like?*

Temple wanted a real hug. But even when she was safe at home,
when her mom leaned down to give her a squeeze,
all she saw was a tidal wave of dentist drills,
sandpaper, and awful cologne coming at her all at once.

Sometimes, when Temple was having a really
bad day, she crawled under the sofa cushions
and asked her little sister to hop on top.
The smoosh of the heavy pillows felt cozy.

Maybe
that's
how hugs worked?

Year after year, Temple filed away images of every hug she came across.

The firefighter coming to the rescue with a ladder and a hug when her neighbor's cat got stuck in a tree.

The teary-eyed couple at the train station, embracing as the whistle blew.

Her little sister, wrapping her arms around their mom . . . just because.

And once, when Temple was in her front yard
building a maze for her pet mouse,
she heard a baby wailing like a fire engine
and looked up to see a mom swaddling
her fussy child in a blanket.

As the mom swayed
back and forth, the cranky baby
instantly hushed.

How do hugs do that?

When she got older, Temple attended
a special boarding school
that gave kids like her a chance to grow.

Temple made friends,
excelled in art and science, won ribbons
for her excellent horseback riding, and . . .

kept building things:
like model rockets,
   a lift for the school's ski slope,
    and a tiny swinging door
for the resident cat
      to go where it pleased.

Around her,
Temple saw families
hug good-bye in September
and hug hello in June.
Temple missed her mom, too,
but she just couldn't express her feelings the same way.

Would she ever get a hug?

At the end of the school year, Temple was invited to spend
the summer at her aunt's ranch in Arizona. Temple kept busy—
drawing and painting, reading books about inventors,
and fixing things around the farm.

She even made a machine
that opened and closed
    the ranch's heavy front gate.

In the yard, Temple
trotted the horses and fed the baby goats,
letting them push up against her hands as they nuzzled for bottles of milk.

She watched newborn calves
take their first wobbly steps
and noticed how they flinched
when tickled by flies.

Just like she did when people tried to touch her!

On the day of the calves' first checkup,
Temple heard frantic mooing and raced outside
to see what the matter was.
A ranch hand was leading a skittish young cow into a mysterious device.

Her aunt explained that the squeeze chute
helped cows stay calm during vet exams.

Temple watched as the
man pressed a lever,

releasing sides
that cradled the animal
in a snug embrace.

Almost immediately, the
nervous calf stopped its lowing
and stood perfectly still.

And suddenly,
Temple had an idea. . . .

She ran to the barn and quickly sketched a plan.
She took measurements and sawed planks.

She found a spool of wire,
a rusty pulley, a length of string,
and some cushions from an old chair.

Would they do what she wanted?

Temple called for her aunt to come see.
Then she crept inside her creation
and pulled on the string
            to let the sides slip around her.

Temple smiled.

The loud noises disappeared.
The air smelled fresh.
And the bright sunshine felt wonderful.

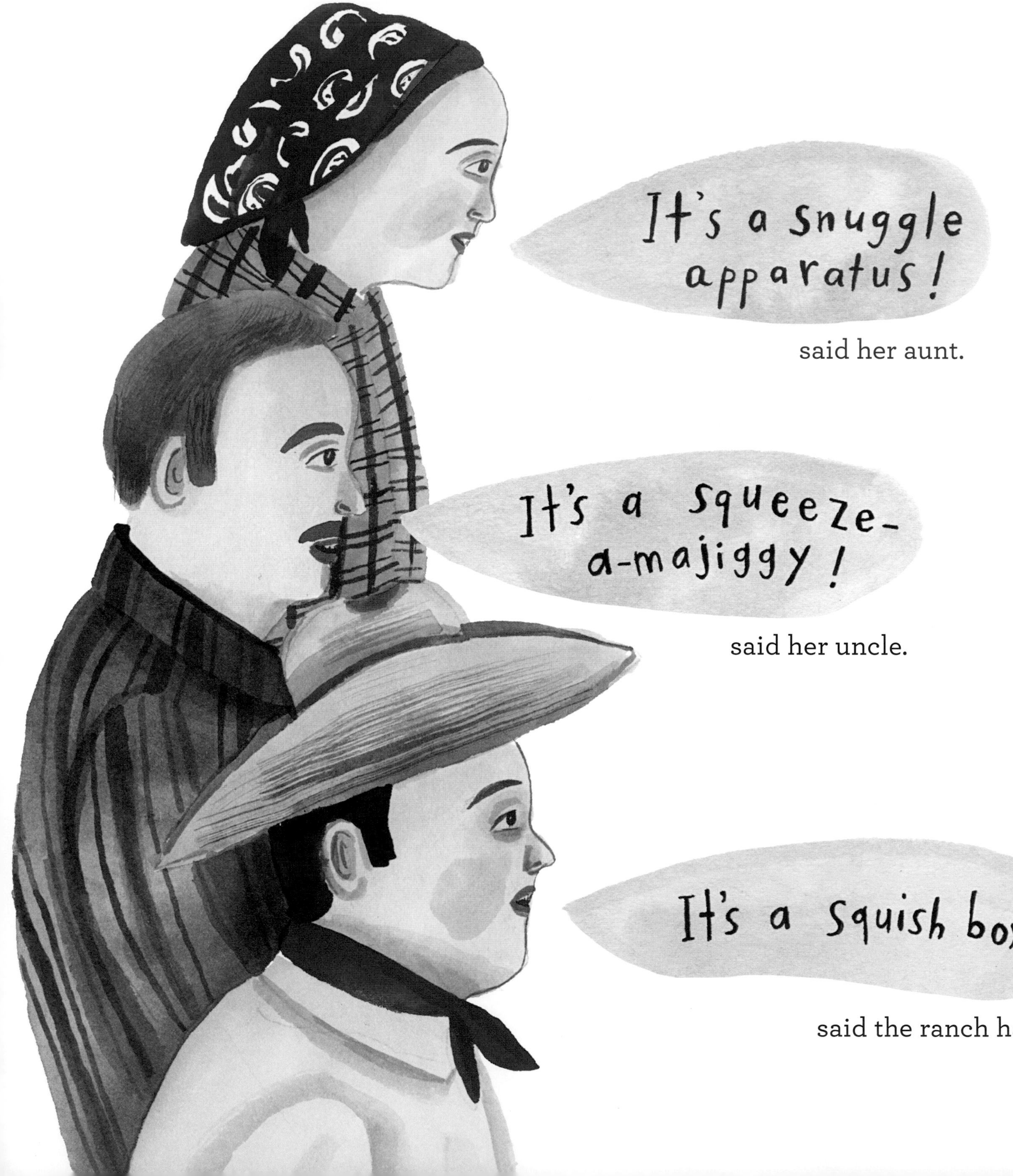

said her aunt.

said her uncle.

said the ranch hand.

Temple brought her invention back home at the end of the summer.

Every time she felt nervous or scared,
she slid inside for a cuddle. But after a while, she began
to use the machine less and less. And then almost not at all.

Then one day, her machine broke . . .

and she knew that only one thing could her cheer her up:

"I'm into hugging people now."
—Temple Grandin

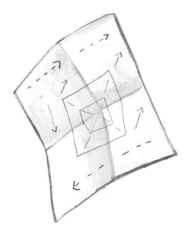

AUTHORS' NOTE

I use my mind to solve problems and invent things.
—Temple Grandin

Dr. Temple Grandin is a professor of animal science at Colorado State University and a leading advocate for the humane treatment of animal livestock. Temple is also known the world over for her courage in speaking out about her personal experience with autism.

Temple was born in Boston, Massachusetts, in 1947, at a time when little was understood about autism. She didn't speak until she was four years old, and even as she grew up, spoken and written languages remained difficult for her. Temple also displayed extreme hypersensitivity to sounds and smells.

But touch, for Temple, was the worst. "Small itches and scratches that most people ignored were torture. . . . Like sandpaper rubbing my skin raw." And giving or getting a hug was impossible. "As a child, I craved to feel the comfort of being held, but I would pull away when people hugged me. When hugged, an overwhelming tidal wave of sensation flowed through me."

What came much easier for Temple—in fact, what came at lightning speed—was an advanced ability to "think in pictures." Everything Temple saw—*snap!*—became a picture in her head that she could recall in vivid detail.

Cheered on by her supportive mother to use her visual thinking to the fullest, Temple loved to draw, paint, sew, and build just about anything—from model airplanes and elaborate kites to lean-tos in the woods behind her house. This was Temple's art and her main way of expressing what made her unique. As Temple told us, "Art was always encouraged in our home. Art was what saved me. Kids need the arts!"

Temple also felt a soothing connection with animals whenever she was around them. She grew up with pet dogs and cats, and even had a pet mouse named Crusader. At the private school she attended in New Hampshire, she took care of the school's stable of horses and became an award-winning rider.

Her love for animals inspired her mother to suggest that Temple spend a summer living with her aunt on her large cattle ranch in Arizona. Temple's experience helping to care for the cattle there laid the foundation for her pioneering work in animal behavior. *Cows understand me and I understand them,* she realized.

When Temple invented her "hug machine" at her aunt's ranch, what she really discovered was that when she was in charge of the timing and pressure of a squeeze, hugs felt wonderful! Temple perfected her hug machine when she returned to school that fall, and like a good scientist, she invited other students to try it out and test its effectiveness. Temple used her hug machine for years. When it finally broke, she realized that she didn't need it anymore.

Temple's story is as unique as she is, and the legacy of her hug machine lives on. Some therapeutic programs for people with autism incorporate deep touch pressure therapy, using devices based on Temple's original designs. As an advocate for people on the autism spectrum, especially children, Temple now travels the globe giving out hugs and inspiring others to embrace what makes them different. "Autism is a part of who I am," she says.

—A. G. and J. T.

For my mom, Judy, who makes beautiful pictures
in her mind and on canvas
—A. G.

For Temple Grandin and Eustacia Cutler;
and to Claire and Chloe, my two favorite huggers
—J. T.

As always, for Pia and Izzy
—G. P.

ATHENEUM
BOOKS FOR YOUNG
READERS • An imprint of Simon &
Schuster Children's Publishing Division • 1230
Avenue of the Americas, New York, New York 10020
• Text copyright © 2018 by Amy Guglielmo and Jacqueline
Tourville • Illustrations copyright © 2018 by Giselle Potter •
Photograph of Temple Grandin on p. 43 copyright © 2018 by Rosalie
Winard • All rights reserved, including the right of reproduction in whole
or in part in any form. • ATHENEUM BOOKS FOR YOUNG READERS is a
registered trademark of Simon & Schuster, Inc. Atheneum logo is a trademark
of Simon & Schuster, Inc. • For information about special discounts for bulk
purchases, please contact Simon & Schuster Special Sales at 1-866-506-1949 or
business@simonandschuster.com. • The Simon & Schuster Speakers Bureau can
bring authors to your live event. For more information or to book an event, contact
the Simon & Schuster Speakers Bureau at 1-866-248-3049 or visit our website at www.
simonspeakers.com. • Book design by Ann Bobco • The text for this book was set
in Archer Medium. • The illustrations for this book were rendered in watercolors. •
Manufactured in China • 0618 SCP • First Edition • 10 9 8 7 6 5 4 3 2 1 • Library
of Congress Cataloging-in-Publication Data • Names: Guglielmo, Amy, author. | Potter,
Giselle, illustrator. • Title: How to build a hug : Temple Grandin and her amazing squeeze
machine / Amy Guglielmo and Jacqueline Tourville ; illustrated by Giselle Potter. •
Description: First edition. | New York : Atheneum Books for Young Readers,
[2018] | Audience: Age 4–8. | Audience: K to Grade 3. • Identifiers: LCCN
2017021314 (print) | ISBN 9781534410978 (hardcover) | ISBN 9781534410985
(eBook) • Subjects: LCSH: Temple, Grandin—Juvenile literature. | Animal
scientists—United States—Biography—Juvenile literature. | Autism
spectrum disorders—Treatment—Juvenile literature. | Autism
spectrum disorders in children—Treatment—Juvenile literature.
| Autism—Patients—Biography—Juvenile literature. |
Autistic children—Biography—Juvenile literature. •
Classification: LCC RC553.A88 G84 2018
(print) | DDC 616.85/8820092 [B]—dc23 •
LC record available at https://
lccn.loc.gov/2017021314

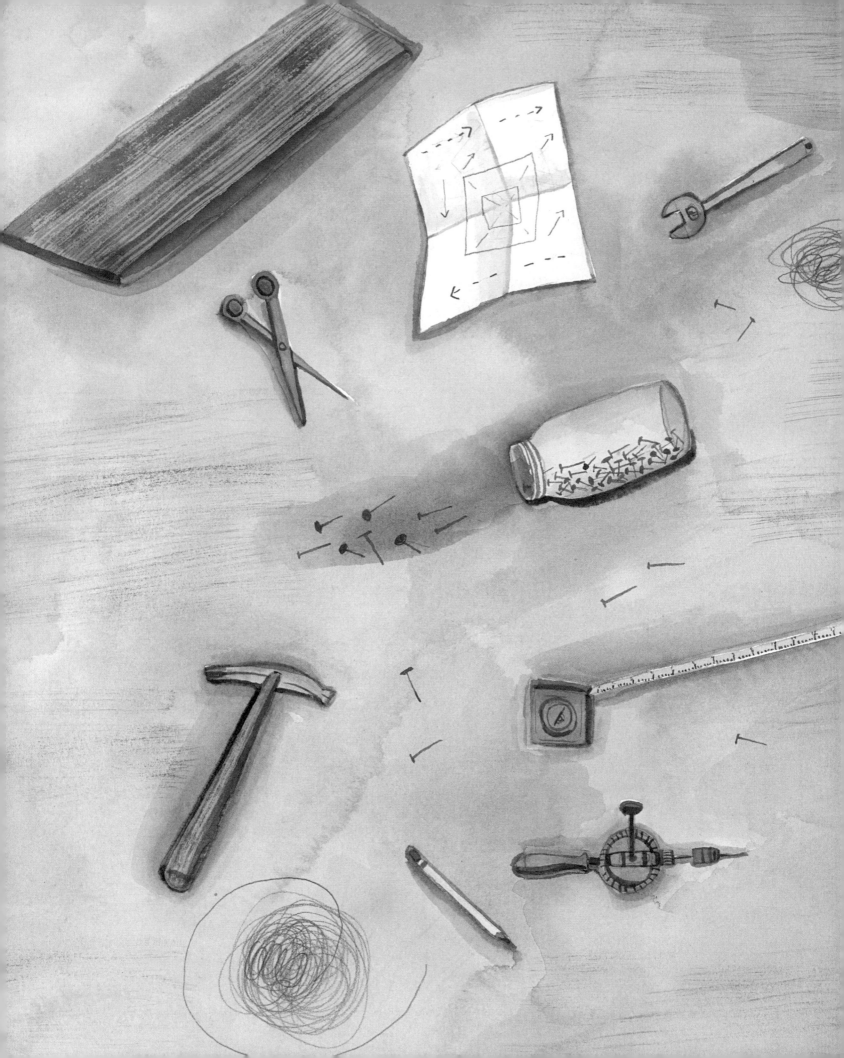